MIDLOTHIAN PUBLIC LIBRARY

3 1614 00189 192

P9-CCG-890

ONE HUNDRED-DOLLAR BILLS

BY MADDIE SPALDING

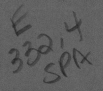

E
3302.4
SPAX

childsworld.com

Published by The Child's World®
1980 Lookout Drive • Mankato, MN 56003-1705
800-599-READ • www.childsworld.com

Photographs ©: Brian McEntire/Shutterstock Images, cover
(foreground), cover (background), 1 (foreground), 1 (background);
iStockphoto, 5, 12–13; Shutterstock Images, 6, 7, 10–11, 20 (top),
20 (bottom); Daniel Azocar/iStockphoto, 9; Kristoffer Tripplaar/
Alamy, 15; Everett Historical/Shutterstock Images, 16; Joe Cicak/
iStockphoto, 19; Red Line Editorial, 22

Design Elements: Brian McEntire/Shutterstock Images; Ben Hodosi/
Shutterstock Images

Copyright © 2018 by The Child's World®
All rights reserved. No part of this book may be reproduced or
utilized in any form or by any means without written permission
from the publisher.

ISBN 9781503820128
LCCN 2016960498

Printed in the United States of America
PA02336

ABOUT THE AUTHOR

Maddie Spalding writes and edits
children's books. She lives in
Minnesota.

TABLE OF CONTENTS

CHAPTER ONE

WHAT IS A ONE HUNDRED-DOLLAR BILL?

One hundred–dollar bills are a type of money. Five twenty-dollar bills equal one one hundred–dollar bill. The Bureau of Engraving and Printing (BEP) makes one hundred–dollar bills. Bills are made from cotton and **linen**.

The BEP makes more than ten billion one hundred–dollar bills each year.

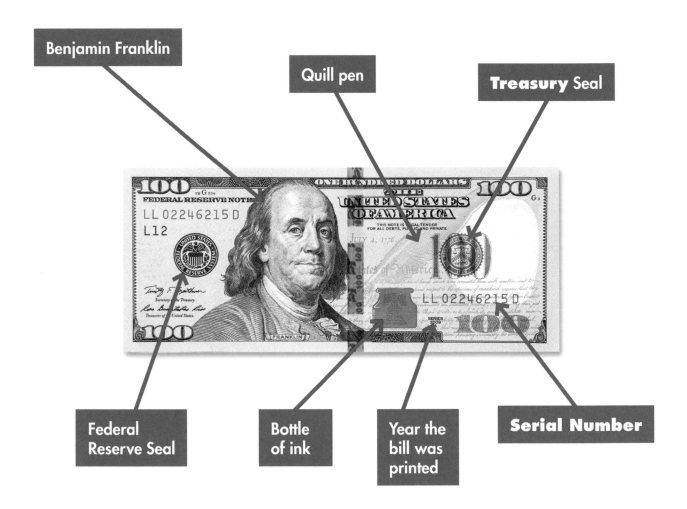

Benjamin Franklin

Quill pen

Treasury Seal

Federal Reserve Seal

Bottle of ink

Year the bill was printed

Serial Number

Benjamin Franklin is on the front of the one hundred–dollar bill.

Why do you think a quill pen and bottle of ink are on the front of the one hundred-dollar bill?

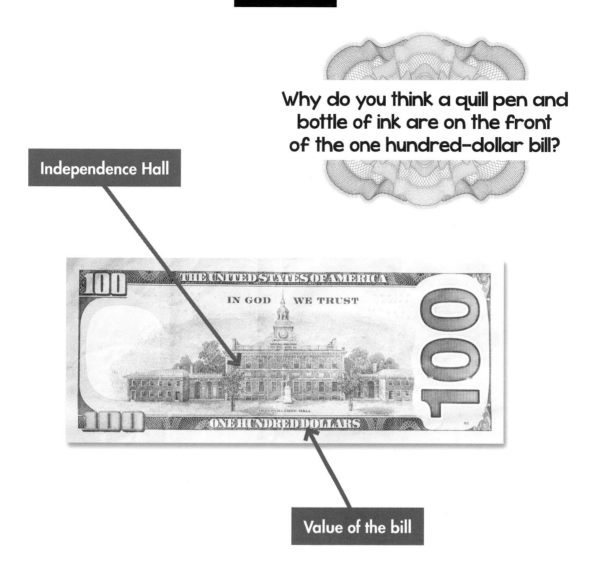

Independence Hall

Value of the bill

Independence Hall is on the back. The Declaration of Independence was signed here.

CHAPTER TWO

SECURITY FEATURES

Each one hundred–dollar bill has a security ribbon. There are pictures of bells in the ribbon. They move when the bill is tilted.

The blue security ribbon is woven into the one hundred–dollar bill's fabric.

The one hundred–dollar bill also has a security thread. This thread glows pink under **ultraviolet** light.

The security thread has USA and the number 100 printed on it.

LF 03263765

SERIES
2009
A

10

The first letter of a serial number identifies the
Federal Reserve Bank that gave out the bill.

12

Each one hundred–dollar bill has a different serial number. These features make it more difficult for people to make fake one hundred–dollar bills.

Which security feature do you think is the most useful? Why?

CHAPTER THREE

THE HISTORY OF THE ONE HUNDRED-DOLLAR BILL

The U.S. government began making one hundred–dollar bills in 1862. An eagle was on the front.

The one hundred–dollar bill was redesigned in 2013.

Abraham Lincoln was the president during the Civil War (1861–1865).

Abraham Lincoln was put on the front of the bill in 1863. He was the 16th president of the United States.

Benjamin Franklin first appeared on the one hundred–dollar bill in 1914. Independence Hall was put on the back of the bill in 1929.

Why might the U.S. government have wanted to put Benjamin Franklin on the one hundred–dollar bill?

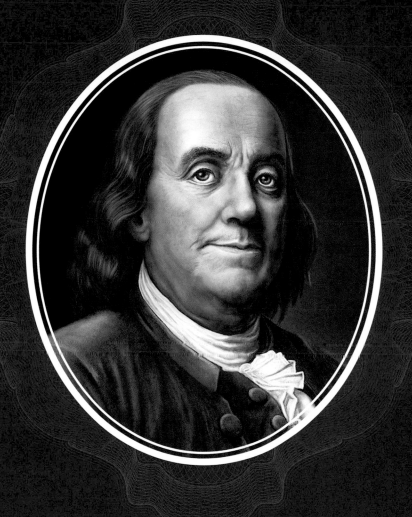

BENJAMIN FRANKLIN

(1706–1790) was an American scientist, author, and inventor. He helped write the Declaration of Independence.

1862 The U.S. government began making one hundred–dollar bills.

1863 Abraham Lincoln was put on the front.

2009 U.S. one hundred–dollar bill

1914 Benjamin Franklin first appeared on the one hundred–dollar bill.

1929 Independence Hall was put on the back of the one hundred–dollar bill.

Back of a 2013 U.S. one hundred–dollar bill

2013 Stronger security features were added to the one hundred–dollar bill.

★ "The United States of America" is written on Benjamin Franklin's jacket collar on the one hundred–dollar bill. But you have to look closely! It is in very small print.

★ The average lifespan of a one hundred–dollar bill is 15 years.

★ The one hundred–dollar bill is the largest bill of value in the United States.

★ The cost to make a one hundred–dollar bill is only 14.3 cents.

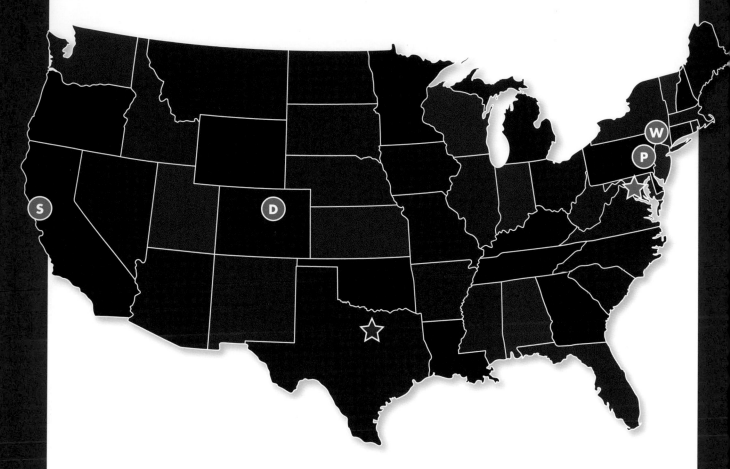

BUREAU OF ENGRAVING AND PRINTING OFFICES

★ Fort Worth, Texas

★ Washington, DC

COIN-PRODUCING MINTS

Ⓓ Denver, Colorado—Produces coins marked with a D.

Ⓟ Philadelphia, Pennsylvania—Produces coins marked with a P.

Ⓢ San Francisco, California—Produces coins marked with an S.

Ⓦ West Point, New York—Produces coins marked with a W.

linen (LIN-uhn) Linen is a strong type of cloth. One hundred–dollar bills are made from cotton and linen.

serial number (SEER-ee-ull NUM-bur) A serial number is a group of numbers that identifies something. Each one hundred–dollar bill has a serial number.

Treasury (TREZH-ur-ee) A Treasury is is in charge of a country's money. The U.S. Department of the Treasury is in charge of money in the United States.

ultraviolet (uhl-truh-VYE-uh-lit) Ultraviolet is a type of light. Security threads on one hundred–dollar bills glow pink under ultraviolet light.

IN THE LIBRARY

Clark, Willow. *The True Story of the Declaration of Independence.* New York, NY: PowerKids, 2013.

Dowdy, Penny. *Money.* New York, NY: Crabtree, 2009.

Jozefowicz, Chris. *10 Fascinating Facts about Dollar Bills.* New York, NY: Children's Press, 2017.

Proudfit, Benjamin. *Benjamin Franklin.* New York, NY: Gareth Stevens, 2015.

ON THE WEB

Visit our Web site for links about one hundred–dollar bills:
childsworld.com/links

Note to Parents, Teachers, and Librarians: We routinely verify our Web links to make sure they are safe and active sites. So encourage your readers to check them out!

INDEX